COMICS BUYER'S GUIDE PRESENTS: THE TEAM!

SENIOR EDITOR
Maggie Thompson

EDITOR
Brent Frankenhoff - ext. 13480
brent.frankenhoff@fwmedia.com

DESIGNER
Jim Butch

ADVERTISING SALES
(800) 726-9966
Steve Madson - ext. 13441
steve.madson@fwmedia.com

AD SALES ASSISTANT
Lori Hauser - ext. 13239

GROUP PUBLISHER
Scott Tappa

EDITORIAL DIRECTOR
Tom Bartsch

F+W MEDIA, INC.
David Nussbaum, Chairman & CEO
James Ogle, CFO
David Blansfield, President
Senior VP, Manufacturing & Production,
Phil Graham
Executive VP, eMedia, Chad Phelps
Senior Vice President of Sales, Dave Davel

Newsstand Circulation
Scott Hill, scott.hill@procirc.com

**TO SUBSCRIBE TO CBG,
CONTACT SUBSCRIBER SERVICES**
(877) 300-0244 or (386) 246-3432
P.O. Box 421651
Palm Coast, FL 32142

EDITORIAL AND AD OFFICE
700 E. State St.
Iola, WI 54990-0001
(715) 445-4612
FAX (715) 445-4087
http://cbgxtra.com
cbg@krause.com

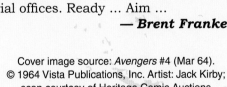

Secret Origins #40 (May 89) © 1989 DC Comics;

Welcome to *Comics Buyer's Guide Presents: The Greatest Comic Book Covers of All Time!* What makes a great cover? Is it the artist, the characters shown, the situation in which they're placed, the age of the buyer, or some other nebulous element or elements? Those were some of the questions we asked ourselves in assembling this, the latest in our *Comics Buyer's Guide Presents* series.

In 1989, then-DC Editor Mark Waid wrote in *Secret Origins* #40 (May 89), "Back in the late 1950s and early 1960s — in the days when we really thought we had the vaguest idea what the hell would really sell a comic book … there were unwritten laws about what to put on a cover. Gorillas, for example — we must have published 200 covers featuring gorillas, probably more. … dinosaurs were popular and sold covers … motorcycles sold. And fires — fires sold … purple covers did well. As did covers with questions-to-the-reader on them … And, last but not least, then-publisher Carmine Infantino swore up and down that if you showed your hero *crying* — well that *made* a cover." Of course, the other factors we discussed also entered our search — and the search even helped define one of the categories. (See if you can guess which one.) Among categories we *didn't* address is the impact of cover logos, including those of DC logo designer Ira Schnapp. What other vital cover elements should we have included? Let us know!

By the way, you should know that *Comics Buyer's Guide* is the longest-running magazine about comics in the Western Hemisphere. Begun in 1971 by a teen in East Moline, Ill., *CBG* has brought comics fans and pros news, reviews, auction updates, and commentary for four decades. Subscription and other information appears on this page, and you can also check out selected back issues free on your mobile device through the Google Newsstand, Comics+, and Graphicly apps.

These were our cover choices. Are they yours? Did we leave out your favorite? Make your case at **CBGXtra.com**, via email to *ohso@krause. com*, or by mail to our editorial offices. Ready … Aim …

— *Brent Frankenhoff*

Published by
Krause Publications, a division of F+W Media, Inc.
700 East State Street • Iola, WI 54990-0001
(715) 445-4612 • (888) 457-2873
www.krausebooks.com
To order books or other products call toll-free 1 (800) 258-0929
or visit us online at www.krausebooks.com

Cover image source: *Avengers* #4 (Mar 64).
© 1964 Vista Publications, Inc. Artist: Jack Kirby;
scan courtesy of Heritage Comic Auctions

ISBN-13: 978-1-4402-3499-6
ISBN-10: 1-4402-3499-X

Cover Design by Jim Butch
Designed by Jim Butch
Edited and written by Brent Frankenhoff and Maggie Thompson
Printed in China

Today, we call the period from approximately 1938 to 1951 the Golden Age, in part because it was when experiments produced a few shining tales that brought riches to the new field of illustrated stories. Many of those early magazines were anthologies, packed with images designed to attract young readers enough that they'd fork over their dimes to support the new art form.

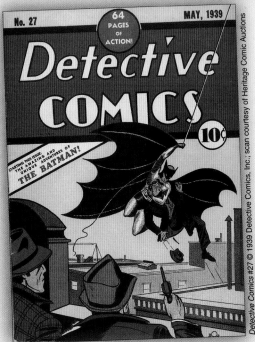

Detective Comics #27 (May 39)
Art by Bob Kane

Less than a year after Superman's debut, DC captured lightning in a bottle again with Batman. Much like his fellow costumed hero, The Dark Knight Detective dominated most covers of this anthology series.

Action Comics #1 (Jun 38)
Art by Joe Shuster

There were costumed adventurers before Superman arrived on the scene, but it was the adventures (and sales) of The Man of Steel that made the super-hero genre explode. Food for thought: Most of the other contents of this new anthology title had been put in place before it was decided to add his story — and this eye-popping cover.

Marvel Comics #1 (Nov 39)
Art by Frank R. Paul

Pulp publisher Martin Goodman expanded into comics with this anthology featuring new characters alongside jungle adventurer Ka-Zar (from his pulps).

More Fun Comics #65 © © 1941 Detective Comics, Inc.

More Fun Comics #65 (Mar 41)
Art by Bernard Bally

What began as a humor anthology, *More Fun Comics* eventually offered the adventures of such fantastic characters as Doctor Fate and The Spectre — which made for a double-take on this cover's combo of words and picture.

Captain America Comics #1 © 1940 Timely Publications

Captain America Comics #1 (Mar 41)
Art by Joe Simon and Jack Kirby

America hadn't yet entered World War II, when Joe Simon and Jack Kirby introduced their star-spangled hero with a U.S. sock to the Führer's jaw.

All-Star Comics #37 © 1947 All-American Comics; scan courtesy of Heritage Comic Auctions

All-Star Comics #37 (Nov 47)
Art by Irwin Hasen

DC's heroes formed a super-team: The Justice Society of America. What worked for the good guys might have worked for the bad. The Injustice Society of the World thought it was worth a try. Readers *had* to check out the results!

> ***Action Comics #1:*** ... let's give him a big S on his chest, and a cape, make him as colorful as we can and as distinctive as we can."
>
> *— Jerry Siegel*
> ***Superman: The Complete History (1998)***

As the art of comics evolved, most publishers stuck to a simple cover format: a company logo, a title, the price, and an eye-catching image. Now and then, companies strayed from that model to make the shopper look twice — and, maybe, buy a copy.

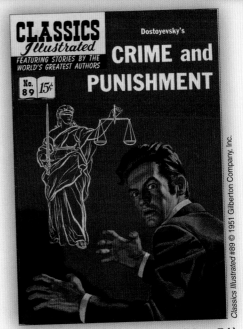

Classics Illustrated #89 (Nov 51)
Art Uncredited

There's no way to tell how many students over the years substituted *Classics* versions for the novels they were supposed to read. This cover, though, aimed to attract casual comics buyers, too. (Those who bought it for English classes may not have known the adaptation ended at the novel's midpoint.)

Extra! #3 (Aug 55)
Art by Johnny Craig

When The Comics Code ended E.C.'s line of weird, crime, and war titles, the publisher tried other genres with its "New Direction" line. This series had a cover design that stood out on the newsstand. *Extra!* featured the adventures of reporters Keith Michaels, Steve Rampart, and Geri Hamilton (another break from the past for a publisher that seldom featured series characters).

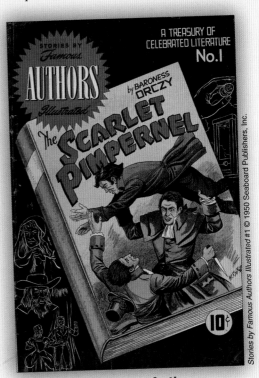

Stories by Famous Authors Illustrated #1 (Aug 50)
Art by H.C. Kiefer

Seaboard attempted to give its adaptations a touch of class with this cover treatment, though the first issue featured an adventure hero.

Secret Six #1 © 1968 National Periodical Publications, Inc.r

Secret Six #1 (May 68)
Art by Frank Springer

Seldom in the history of newsstand comics has a comic book begun its story on the front cover of the issue. Was it a successful marketing tool? Well, it was a mystery novel that was canceled before the mystery was solved.

Superman: The Man of Steel #30 © 1993 DC Comics

Superman: The Man of Steel #30 (Feb 94)
Art by Jon Bogdanove

Hailed as the "first-ever do-it-yourself cover," it featured a sheet of vinyl clings of Superman and Lobo in an assortment of poses that readers could stick to the cover to stage their own fights.

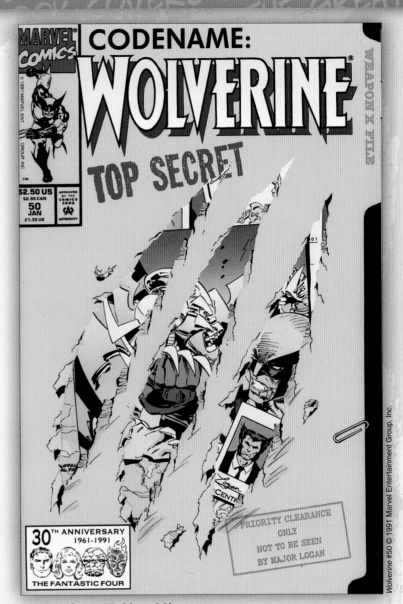

Wolverine #50 © 1991 Marvel Entertainment Group, Inc.

Wolverine #50 (Jan 92)
Art by Marc Silverstri and Dan Green

After years of teases about Wolverine's past, this issue revealed key points of information under its "shredded file folder" cover.

Extra! #3: I liked it because it was a clean type of story, and clean type of book … it had an engaging character, someone whom I could develop and build on.

— *Johnny Craig*
Interview with art collector Roger Hill, 1969
Reprinted from Foul Play!, 2005

One way a cover grabs readers is by tantalizing them with a crisis so compelling that they must buy the issue to see how it's resolved. To pull it off, the artist packs the image with tension — and a story clearly told.

Mister Mystery #12 (Aug 53)
Art by Bernard Baily

The potential of serious eye injury was an element in more than one story in the 1940s and 1950s. In fact, it was singled out as offensive — and *that* meant some collectors actually began (pardon the expression) keeping an eye out for such issues.

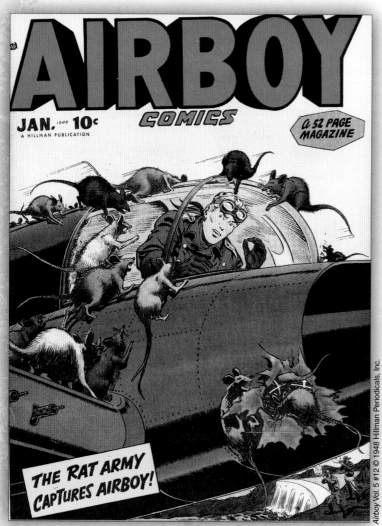

Airboy Vol. 5 #12 (#59, Jan 49)
Art by Dan Zolnerowich

Readers had already read the first part of the two-part tale of "Airboy and the Rats," so they should have been eager to grab this second installment anyway. Nevertheless, this cover was designed to attract even more buyers to a story that suggested that, if the world's rats could unite to attack mankind, it might be impossible to defeat them. It was nightmare time.

Strange Suspense Stories #19 (Jul 54)
Art by Steve Ditko

Eeeek! *Now* what?

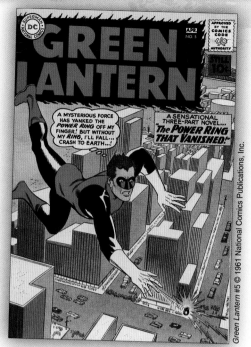

Green Lantern #5 (Apr 61)
Art by Gil Kane and Joe Giella

OK, tricky enough dealing with one super-villain after another. But without his power ring? Hey, it'll only take a dime to find out how he gets out of this — *if* he does!

Flash #163 (Aug 66)
Art by Carmine Infantino and Joe Giella

Breaking the Fourth Wall? Yep, it's *that* serious for Barry Allen! Well, if fans are true blue, they should be willing to fork over 12¢ to demonstrate their loyalty, right? What's with him, anyway?

Thor #364 (Feb 86)
Art by Walter Simonson

It was not only an unusual Thor story by Walter Simonson. It was also, as other covers used to proclaim, "Not a dream, a hoax, or an imaginary story!" What the heck? Who could pass *this* up?

Strange Suspense Stories #19: Charlton was the lord of low-budget comics, but it did publish many good issues.

— *Tony Isabella*
1000 Comic Books You Must Read, 2009

Speaking of imaginary stories (which we were on page 7, you may recall): In "Whatever Happened to The Man of Tomorrow?," Alan Moore explained that *all* comics stories are "imaginary tales," but that *these* are the stories in which the usual rules don't apply and the status quo can change radically. So why would anyone bother with them, if they make no difference? Or are we overthinking this? What do you *mean*, "Could be"?

Superman #149 (Nov 61)
Art by Curt Swan and Stan Kaye

The Man of Steel would die — or at least come perilously close to meeting his maker — multiple times in the 1960s. World Color Press probably had to stock up on components of green ink for all the times Superman was poisoned by green kryptonite.

Superman's Girl Friend Lois Lane #19 (Aug 60)
Art by Curt Swan and Stan Kaye

Editor Mort Weisinger introduced the concept of Imaginary Tales with the first story of "Mr. and Mrs. Superman." More imaginary than the marriage of Clark Kent and Lois Lane was Lois' wardrobe for a simple dinner at home. Move over, Donna Reed! (*Editor Maggie's note:* That's Editor Brent writing, folks. He's too young to know about the Gracious Living that was home life in almost *all* of 1960s pop culture.)

Superman #162 (Jul 63)
Art by Kurt Schaffenberger

Kurt Schaffenberger's cover gave readers two Supermen for the price of one — as well as an easy way to tell them apart. (Some remember the tale fondly; some were just bored by one big happy ending. But it's classic.)

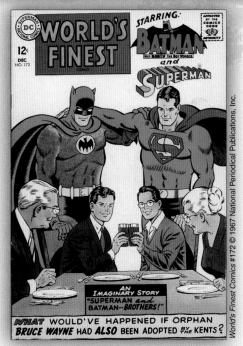

World's Finest Comics #172 (Dec 67)
Art by Curt Swan and George Klein

Changes to their origin stories were another
staple of Imaginary Stories featuring Superman
and Batman. The concept would return in DC's
Elseworlds titles in the 1980s and '90s.

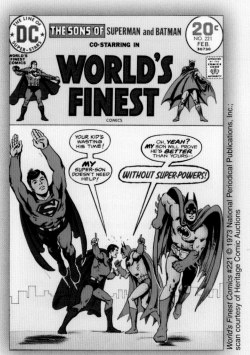

World's Finest Comics #221 (Feb 74)
Art by Nick Cardy

Following an earlier series of super-offspring
one-shot adventures, the "Super-Sons" stories
began with a Nick Cardy cover and a fun switch
on the "my dad can beat up your dad" idea.

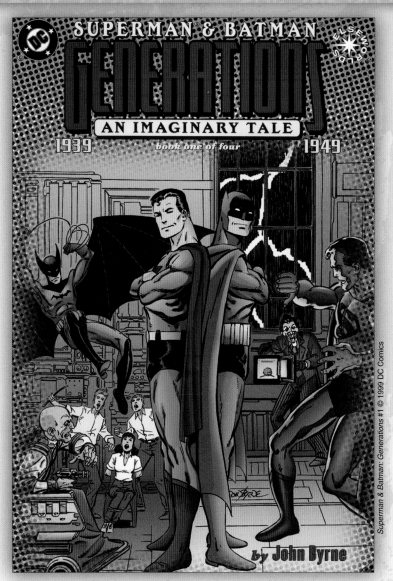

Superman & Batman: Generations #1 (1999)
Art by John Byrne

John Byrne took The Man of Steel and The Dark Knight through the
decades, allowing each to age, have children, and face the challenges
that age can bring in an imaginative mini-series. He flawlessly captured
the look of the characters in each decade of their appearance.

> **World's Finest Comics #172:** I think
> this Curt Swan/George Klein cover may
> have been on the first comic book I ever
> read. I loved having my two favorite
> heroes together in the same family in this
> imaginary story.
>
> — *Norm Breyfogle*
> *CBG #1677, May 2011*

Especially just before and during World War II, American magazines sought out powerful images to display support of the nation. Though use of such images have been less frequent in the years since, they can still attract readers.

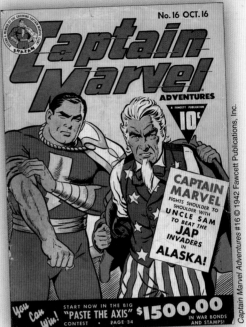

Captain Marvel Adventures #16 (Oct 42)
Art by C.C. Beck

Once the U.S. was in World War II, it was time for everyone to roll up their sleeves and get to work, as Captain Marvel and Uncle Sam demonstrated. One way kids could "Paste the Axis," by the way, was by buying war bonds — a message that was often repeated throughout the conflict.

Superman #14 (Jan 42)
Art by Fred Ray

Already clothed in red and blue, Superman was a natural candidate for patriotic covers, including this Fred Ray example. Several *CBGXtra. com* readers cited it, when we asked them to suggest comics' greatest covers.

Captain Marvel Jr. #21 (Jul 44)
Art by Mac Raboy

And there was no need to be subtle about war bonds and stamps. In fact, covers indicated it was simply a happy thing to do.

Doll Man Quarterly #6 (Sum 43)
Art by Al Bryant

Striking cover images made matters clear.

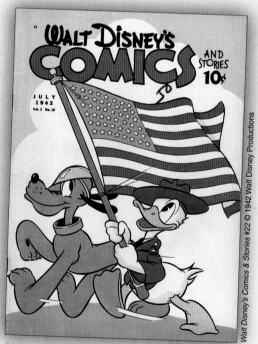

Walt Disney's Comics & Stories #22 (Jul 42)
Art by Carl Buettner

Even funny animals flew the flag during the war.

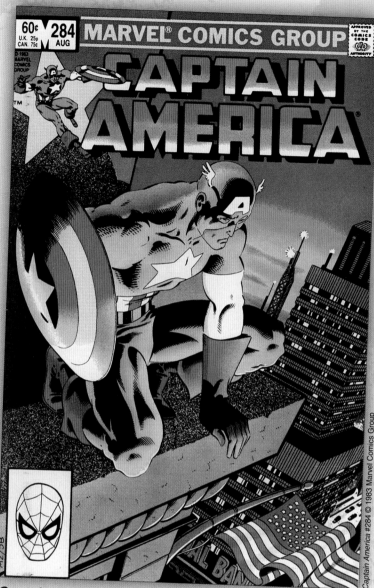

Captain America #284 (Aug 83)
Art by Mike Zeck and John Beatty

This introspective image was reused as the cover for **Comics Buyer's Guide** #1455 in 2001, following the September 11 attacks. A powerful image is a powerful image — and sometimes editors simply find that a powerful image is the best way to express a compelling emotion that will be shared by readers.

Superman #14: With that eagle on his arm and the star-spangled shield behind him, has any cover ever done a better job of saying, "Truth, Justice, and the American Way"?

— *Len Wein*
CBG #1608, September 2005

Jack Kirby created this iconic image to kick off what became known as The Marvel Age of Comics with *Fantastic Four* #1 (Nov 61). It has inspired other artists to create their own versions in the years since. A true swipe should be a stolen image passed off as an original creation. In the case of the covers on these pages, each is clearly designed to recall to the reader the original Kirby creation. Take a gander at the characters other covers have substituted for the roles of Mr. Fantastic, The Thing, The Human Torch, and The Invisible Girl.

Fantastic Four #126 (Sep 72)
Art by John Buscema and Joe Sinnott

A retelling of the team's origin was a good excuse to present a new rendition of the original cover.

Fantastic Four #1 (Nov 61)
Art by Jack Kirby

Prior to this issue, Marvel (then known as Atlas) was best known for its monster comics. It's no surprise that this first pass at a new line of super-hero titles stayed close to those earlier tales of menace.

Marvel Age #14 (May 84)
Art by John Byrne

Longtime *Fantastic Four* artist and writer John Byrne put himself into the act in one of his variations on the original theme.

Avengers West Coast #54 (Jan 90)
Art by John Byrne

John Byrne provided another homage and even added a few more characters.

Married ... with Children:
Quantum Quartet #1 (Oct 93)
Art by Tom Richmond and David Mowry

The Bundys somehow acquired super-powers in this short-lived mini-series.

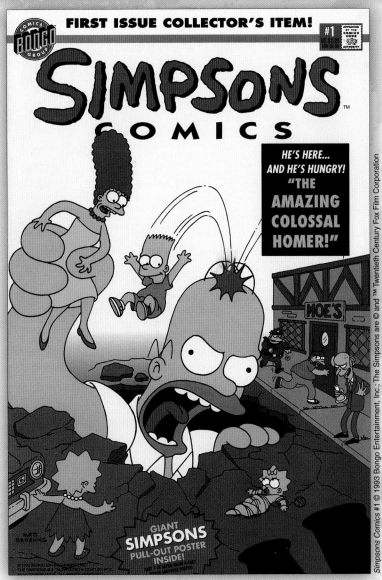

Simpsons Comics #1 (1993)
Art by Bill Morrison

The long-running series starring Springfield's favorite dysfunctional family has had a number of super-hero homage covers. How appropriate that this "first issue collector's item" was a tribute to the 1961 classic! (And, hey, a bonus pull-out poster! Who could resist?)

***Fantastic Four* #1:** My brother Frank read me this issue several times when I was 3 and 4 years old. When I was 6, he gave it to me for Christmas.

— *John Verzyl*
CBG #1649, January 2009

A second age of super-heroes dawned in late 1956 with an updated version of DC's Flash. DC quickly followed The Scarlet Speedster with other re-imagined versions of its Golden Age heroes. Soon, as DC's success became apparent, other publishers began revivals of their own. The Silver Age of Comics, which collectors have established as roughly 1956-1971, was a second era of super-heroic imagination — both in storytelling and in presentation.

Amazing Fantasy #15 (Aug 62)
Art by Jack Kirby and Steve Ditko

Mild-mannered nerd Peter Parker made his first appearance in the final issue of an anthology title. The experiment of editor-writer Stan Lee and artist Steve Ditko paid off. (Marvel at the awesome might, indeed! Note the cover plug for the upcoming series.)

Showcase #4 (Oct 56)
Art by Carmine Infantino and Joe Kubert

DC's reintroduction of The Flash began a revival of super-heroes that, within a few years, spawned The Marvel Age of Comics (beginning with *Fantastic Four #1*). The Flash's super-speed power was emphasized by its cover "capture" on high-speed film, and the story paid tribute to earlier years with the hero's reading an issue of *Flash Comics*.

Adventure Comics #247 (Apr 58)
Art by Curt Swan and Stan Kaye

Kids' clubs have been around since the first children met in the back of the cave. What could be more cool than a club with Superboy? Wait! *No?* What was up with that?

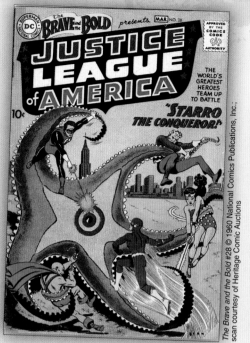

The Brave and the Bold #28 (Mar 60)
Art by Mike Sekowsky and Murphy Anderson

Remembering the success of DC's Justice Society, Editor and Yankees fan Julius Schwartz teamed DC's newly revived heroes into a League.

The Flash #123 (Sep 61)
Art by Carmine Infantino and Murphy Anderson

Two Flashes on two Earths opened multiple story possibilities while causing headaches for continuity cops. That said, it was a spectacular story that *did* "become a classic!"

Avengers #4 (Mar 64)
Art by Jack Kirby and George Roussos

Marvel's most popular Golden Age character came to the Silver Age and was retroactively inducted as an Avengers charter member. Many today recall Jack Kirby's hard-charging cover with fondness. (Check out our Top 10 on Page 61.)

The Brave and the Bold #28: The "Just Imagine ..." house ad for this that thrilled me and hundreds of thousands of other young readers was probably my most memorable comic-book experience.

— *Dave Gibbons*
CBG #1612, January 2006

I t all began with Alan Scott and a magical green lantern (think Aladdin) that gave him power over almost anything except (yes) wood. When the Silver Age revisited the concept, it was with Hal Jordan, member of an science-fictional peacekeeping force with power over almost anything except (yes) the color yellow. There have been a variety of GLs — and their ups and downs — ever since. Each has faced challenges (and appeared on cool covers).

All-American Comics #95 (Mar 48)
Art by Carmine Infantino

Can't you just hear GL saying to Harlequin, "I'll show you mine if you show me yours!"? (And ignoring all the crooks and cops blazing away at each other.)

Green Lantern #1 (Sep 41)
Art by Howard Purcel

Alan Scott got his start as the first Green Lantern in *All-American Comics* #16 (Jul 40). By the next year, sales warranted the addition of his own title, and this cover made the concept clear: powerful lantern, action, and adventure.

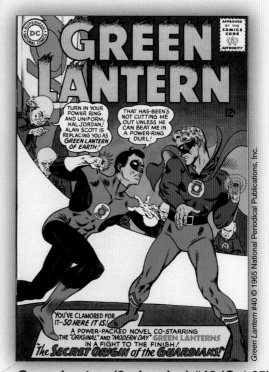

Green Lantern (2nd series) #40 (Oct 65)
Art by Gil Kane and Murphy Anderson

If Alan Scott replaced Hal Jordan in the Earth-1 universe, who would take up Alan's role in the Earth-2 universe? Those darn Guardians didn't always think things through, but readers wanted to see it.

Green Lantern (2nd series) #76
(Apr 70)
Art by Neal Adams

The cover made it clear when writer Denny
O'Neil and artist Neal Adams teamed Green
Lantern and Green Arrow to move the series
from super-hero conflicts to social ones.

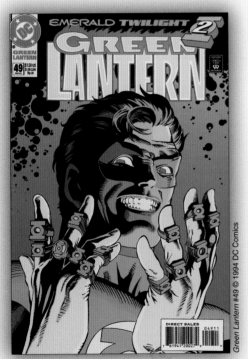

Green Lantern (3rd series) #49
(Feb 94)
Art by Darryl Banks and Romeo Tanghal

If one infinitely powerful power ring is good,
how much better would a dozen more be?
Cool concept, clearly conveyed!

Green Lantern (4th series) #1 (Jul 05)
Art by Carlos Pacheco and Jesus Merino

Carlos Pacheco and Jesus Merino's cover for a relaunched Green
Lantern series made it clear that Hal Jordan is the Greatest. Green
Lantern. Ever.

> ***Green Lantern*** (2nd series) #76:
> Single-color covers are always arresting,
> especially when, as with this one, there's
> a content reason.
>
> — *Andrew "Captain Comics" Smith*
> *CBG #1617, June 2006*

Every now and then in the history of comics, artists have sneaked in *double-entendre* images that many readers missed. In some cases, even the *editor* missed the gag until after the issue had come off the press. In other cases, what was once an innocent cover or phrase can now induce laughter in a modern reader.

Tense Suspense #1 (Dec 58)
Art by Dick Ayers

If this cover featured *Seinfeld*'s George Costanza, he would be protesting that it was shrinkage.

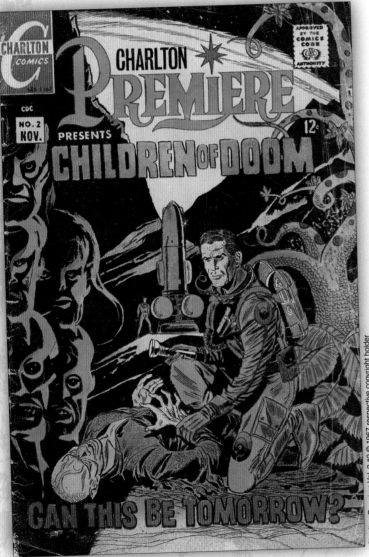

Charlton Premiere Vol. 2 #2 (Nov 67)
art by Pat Boyette

Artist Pat Boyette wasn't the first to include a phallic symbol on a cover, and he certainly won't be the last. If you say, "Blast off!" you should be ashamed of yourself. (By the way, the story "Children of Doom" by Boyette and writer Denny O'Neil is considered a classic in the field.)

Eh! #4 (Jun 54)
Art by Fred Ottenheimer

We'll let you build the mighty, mighty joke here.

ALF #48 (Dec 91)
Art by Dave Manak

What can we say? Talk about 100% fresh!

The Rifleman #10 (Mar 62)

OK, this is just a strange camera angle combined with similarly strange expressions and props. Let's say no more about it.

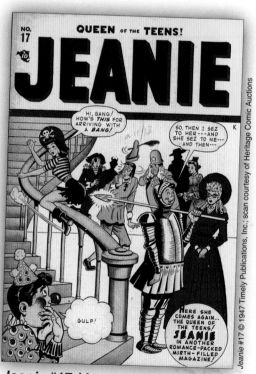

Jeanie #17 (Jan 48)
Art uncredited

Despite any appearances to the contrary, we're pretty sure this is an innocent costume party.

***The Rifleman* #10:** Would somebody please call protective services? Mark needs help — or does he?

— ***Vincent Zurzolo***
CBG #1662, February 2010

W hat began as "Educational Comics," producing such titles as *Picture Stories from the Bible* and *Tiny Tot Comics,* used the same initials to add its "Entertaining Comics" line. The resultant combo produced some of the most memorable comics of the early 1950s — and some of the most startling images.

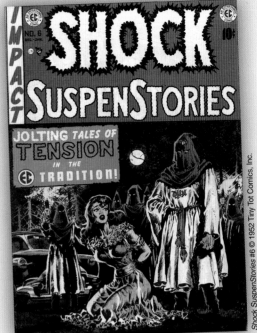

Shock SuspenStories #6 (Jan 53)
Art by Wally Wood

E.C. crusaded for civil rights and the end of hate groups. It demonstrated that social commentary could provide captivating imagery, as in this thinly veiled take on the Ku Klux Klan.

Crime SuspenStories #22 (May 54)
Art by Johnny Craig

When asked during a Congressional hearing if he considered this cover to be in "good taste," E.C. Publisher William Gaines said that it was good taste, "for the cover of a horror comic. A cover in bad taste, for example, might be defined as holding the head a little higher so that the neck could be seen dripping blood from it and moving the body over a little further so that the neck of the body could be seen to be bloody."

Tales from the Crypt #28 (Mar 52)
Art by Al Feldstein

Years before, artist Harry Clarke had illustrated Edgar Allan Poe's tale of premature burial. E.C. often used other works as inspiration, and this Clarke-based image was sure to attract buyers — and nightmares.

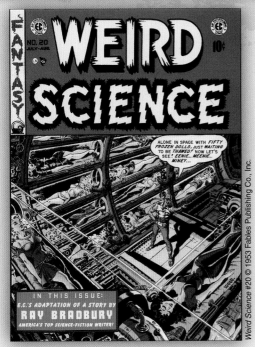

Weird Science #20 (Aug 53)
Art by Wally Wood

Be careful what you wish for, even if it *is* a spaceship full of beautiful women as drawn by Wally Wood. (Note the plug for a Ray Bradbury story; the writer's agreement with the publisher regarding comics adaptations brought fans to comics and comics to fans.)

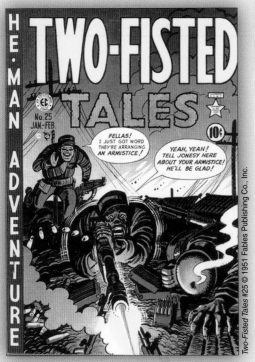

Two-Fisted Tales #25 (Feb 52)
Art by Harvey Kurtzman

Editor, writer, and artist Harvey Kurtzman made social commentary "must" reading, whether in E.C.'s war titles or in *Mad*.

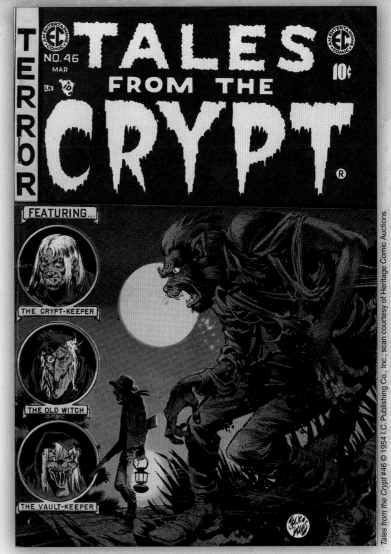

Tales from the Crypt #46 (Mar 55)
Art by Jack Davis

Readers familiar with Jack Davis' work on a variety of mass-market-magazine covers might have been taken aback to realize he was also a master of creative horror-comics covers.

Crime SuspenStories #22: A cover in bad taste, for example, might be defined as holding the head a little higher so that the neck could be seen dripping blood from it …

— *William Gaines*
Testimony before Congressional hearing, 1954

The Man of Steel provided such a powerful image that he virtually defined what readers sought in heroic fantasy. He began by appearing on two of the first eight issues of *Action Comics*. By #9, the publisher put a promise on every cover that he would appear in the issue — and, by #19, the series simply featured Superman on every cover, by #24 (May 40) claiming to be the "world's largest selling comic magazine!" His cover appearance was enough to say, "This comic book is about heroism, adventure, and power."

Superboy #47 (Mar 56)
Art by Curt Swan and Stan Kaye

If Superman is almost infinitely powerful as an adult, how close to infinitely powerful was he as a boy? Readers wanted to know — and this issue might provide the answer!

Superman #1 (Sum 39)
Art by Joe Shuster

The first DC character to receive his own title, Superman looked to be jumping for joy on this cover. What more did the issue need to entice readers already trained to look for "the one and only Superman"?

Superman #32 (Feb 45)
Art by Wayne Boring

The sheer *fun* of having super-powers came through on this Wayne Boring cover.

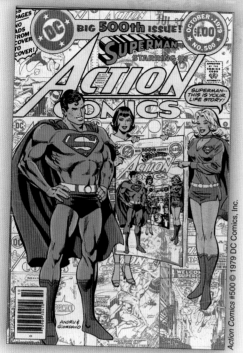

Action Comics #500 (Oct 79)
Art by Curt Swan

It took just over 40 years, but *Action Comics* was the first comic book to reach the magic 500-issue mark. DC rewarded readers with an anniversary issue and a cover displaying significant events from the series' past.

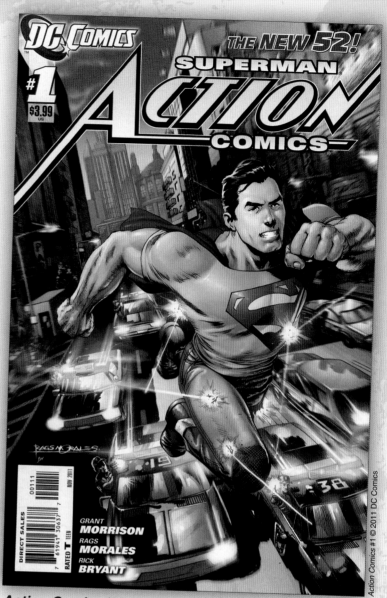

Action Comics (2nd series) #1 (Nov 11)
Art by Rags Morales

Rags Morales demonstrates how the (again!) newly revamped Superman functions early in his career in DC's re-imagined universe. He's returned to the social-crusader roots he had in the Golden Age. (Note to ponder: Might *Action Comics* resume its *original* numbering, as it approaches #1,000 in a few years?)

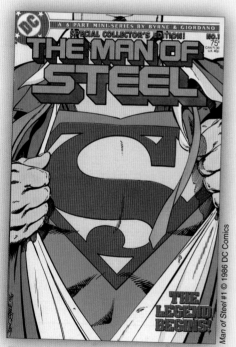

The Man of Steel #1 (1986)
Art by John Byrne

John Byrne's revamp of Superman retained the character's iconic symbol on this alternate cover. Byrne described the optical illusion he saw when he looked at Superman's chest as "two yellow fish swimming past each other."

> ***Superman* #1:** It's an iconic cover to introduce an iconic character.
>
> — *Maggie Thompson*
> *CBG #1609, October 2005*

Today, most monthly comics are aimed at customers old enough to vote. (Face it: Buyers have to have a pretty good income to shell out enough cash to follow all their favorites these days.) But a few decades ago, the customers could manage a dime here or there — and the publishers targeted that market with gags and characters that resonated with readers.

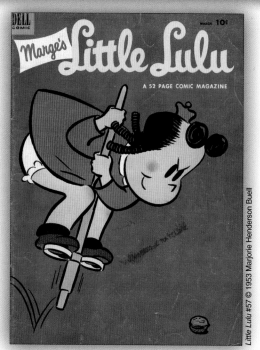

Little Lulu #57 (Mar 53)
Art by John Stanley

Writer-artist John Stanley transformed Marjorie Henderson Buell's Lulu from the star of one-panel gags to the lead character in wildly imaginative multi-page stories. But his covers, of course, had to be one-panel gags of their own.

Four-Color Comics #199 (Oct 48)
Art by Carl Barks

Square eggs? Square chickens? What did Donald and the boys stumble into this time? Readers of all ages had to pick up the issue to find out. And the story — written and drawn by Carl Barks — was so memorable that those readers were still talking about it years later, when they'd grown up.

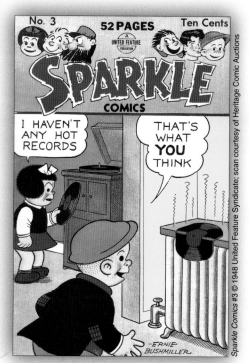

Sparkle Comics #3 (Feb 49)
Art by Ernie Bushmiller

Disguised as a joke, there was actually a lesson here for readers. (We can only hope the scientifically minded kids didn't similarly experiment with their parents' discs.)

Four-Color Comics #223 (Apr 49)
Art by Carl Barks

With Westerns playing every Saturday at local theaters, it was natural to put Donald and the kids in a Western adventure story. Well, a Western adventure story with ducks.

Supersnipe Comics Vol. 1 #7 (Jan 43)
Art by George Marcoux

Some people think comics collecting didn't begin until the 1960s — but Supersnipe resonated with many young readers. Which, of course, is exactly what the publisher hoped.

Sugar & Spike #17 (Aug 58)
Art by Sheldon Mayer

Sheldon Mayer's toddlers had their own view of the world, based on their limited experiences. The gimmick that hooked young readers was that they could feel smarter than Sugar and Spike, because the reader knew what was going on. The toddlers, on the other hand, could only talk baby talk and were often bewildered by the world around them.

Four Color Comics #223: Wonder and absurdity blend in an adventure many consider the best Donald Duck tale of all.
— *Tony Isabella*
1000 Comic Books You Must Read, 2009

The World's Mightiest Mortal, also known as Captain Marvel, was a Golden Age great. Newscaster Billy Batson was granted the powers of an odd blend of classic characters when he spoke the magic word made up of their initials (Solomon, Hercules, Atlas, Zeus, Achilles, and Mercury). The boy Billy and his Marvel Family were wish fulfillment writ large for thousands of adoring fans. (More than one kid tried a variety of pronunciations in hopes of — Well, you never know, do you?)

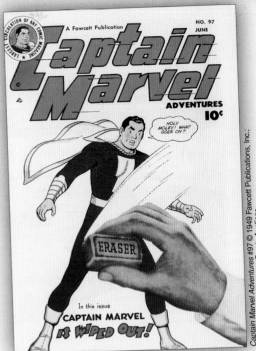

Captain Marvel Adventures #97
(Jun 49)
Art by C.C. Beck

Whether or not that was the hand of primary Captain Marvel artist C.C. Beck that was erasing the hero is unknown. But the best way to find out what was going on was to buy the issue. Of course.

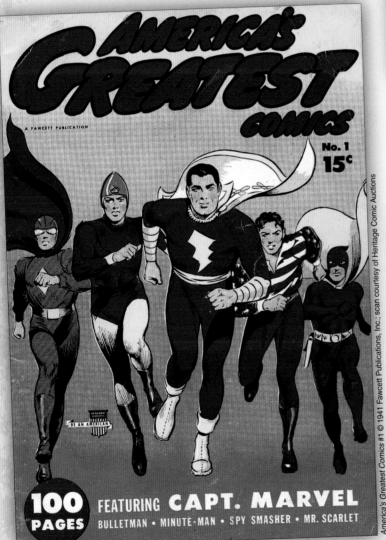

America's Greatest Comics #1 (1941)
Art by Mac Raboy

Fawcett didn't hide its light under a bushel with this title, which provided a showcase for, not only Captain Marvel, but also other Fawcett Universe heroes. It was a little pricey at 15¢, but gee! 100 pages!

Master Comics #32 (Nov 42)
Art by Mac Raboy

Mac Raboy produced many Captain Marvel Jr. covers for Fawcett. Did you know the character design was so good that Elvis Presley patterned his hairstyle on Junior?

Marvel Family #7 © 1946 Fawcett Publications, Inc.; scan courtesy of Heritage Comic Auctions

Marvel Family #7 (Dec 46)
Art by C.C. Beck and Pete Costanza

The three main Marvels joined forces in the aptly named *Marvel Family*. This issue featured them visiting their point of origin: Why? Readers knew something *vital* had to be at stake.

Mary Marvel #5 © 1946 Fawcett Publications, Inc.

Mary Marvel #5 (Sep 46)
Art by Jack Binder

This beautiful cover by Jack Binder (brother of Marvel Family stories writer Otto Binder) was later used as a "color by numbers" page in a large reprint volume in the 1970s.

Power of Shazam #1 © 1995 DC Comics

Power of Shazam! #1 (Mar 95)
Art by Jerry Ordway

Jerry Ordway reimagined Captain Marvel for the post-"Crisis on Infinite Earths" DC Universe with many nods to the Marvel Family's Golden Age adventures. Even the cover of the first issue features elements of Captain Marvel's origin in *Whiz Comics* #2 (Feb 40).

> **Master Comics #32:** For many comic art fans, few works are finer than a Mac Raboy Captain Marvel Jr.
> — *Heritage Comic Auctions Comics Signature Sale catalog, Aug. 13, 2005*

The death of a character, no matter how major or minor, is always a loss to that character's fans. On the other hand, issues that promise a death sometimes see a boost in sales (even though seasoned fans are often skeptical). Superman *really* dies this time? For *sure*? Well …

Giant-Size Avengers #3 (Feb 75)
Art by Gil Kane and Frank Giacoia

The Vision's warning clearly challenged readers to pick up the issue to see which character (or characters) would shuffle off their mortal coil (or coils). (Don't worry. They got better.) What the heck? Why not buy it?

Uncanny X-Men #142 (Feb 81)
Art by Terry Austin

Wow! This must mean the end of the popular title! Right? I said, "*Right?*" Yeah, despite the cover's hyperbole, everyone *didn't* die, not even in the possible future in which the Sentinels ruled. Cool cover, though — no?

Superman #156 (Oct 62)
Art by Curt Swan and George Klein

Oh, that pesky Virus X. It would return to plague The Man of Steel later in the '60s. Would readers remember that it had laid Superman low? And it had been (gasp!) *real*!

Action Comics #399 (Apr 71)
Art by Neal Adams

"What I tell you three times is true!" Yikes! Better hope not, Man of Steel! And what the heck were Doom-Bells? Better buy that issue to find out!

Marvel Graphic Novel #1: *The Death of Captain Marvel* (1982)
Art by Jim Starlin

Jim Starlin wrapped up the cosmic adventures of Marvel's Captain Marvel with the hero laid low. The powerful story featured a powerful cover, evoking Michelangelo's *Pieta*.

Flash #186 (Mar 69)
Art by Ross Andru and Mike Esposito

Now, this sort of cover is just plain yucky — but DC has featured it from time to time. After all, what spells d-e-a-t-h more clearly than a skeletal figure in a hero's costume? Hot dog! Who *wouldn't* want to buy a comic book with a decayed hero on the cover?

Not dead-dead. COMICS-dead.
— *Glen Weldon*
@ghweldon Twitter (Jan 25 11)

"Sex sells." Many comics publishers endorsed the concept and hoped to demonstrate its truth from the Golden Age to today. Many costumes were tight and/or revealing. Moreover, while free Sears catalogs did contain underwear displays, for a dime more, comic books provided the bonus of adventure and plot. Wowza, right? (Is this a good time to mention that our *next* edition of **CBG** *Presents* will be *Dangerous Curves*?)

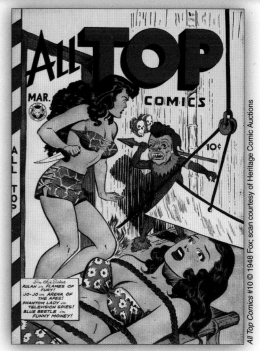

All-Top Comics #10 (Mar 48)
Art by Jack Kamen

Despite the title, the characters are all wearing bottoms, as well (even if both tops and bottoms are skimpy). It may be hot in the jungle, but were these outfits really practical?

Phantom Lady #17 (Apr 48)
Art by Matt Baker

Discuss "comics cheesecake" with any longtime fan, and chances are that this Matt Baker image will be mentioned. It was also one of the examples cited in Fredric Wertham's *Seduction of the Innocent*, which complained that such material should not be permitted in comic books.

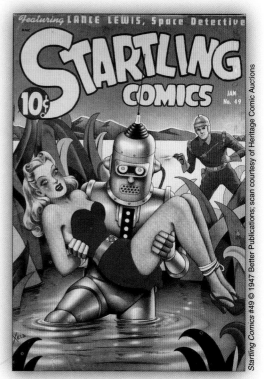

Startling Comics #49 (Jan 48)
Art by Alex Schomburg

Alex Schomburg may be best known for his busy covers for Timely, but he could also produce exciting covers without so many elements.

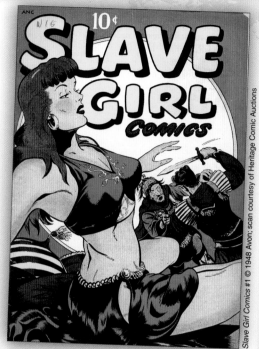

Slave Girl Comics #1 (Feb 49)

Art by Howard Larsen

Avon pulled no punches with the title and cover art for this one. In the course of its comics publishing, it experimented with a variety of genres, managing success with few. This series, for example, lasted only two issues.

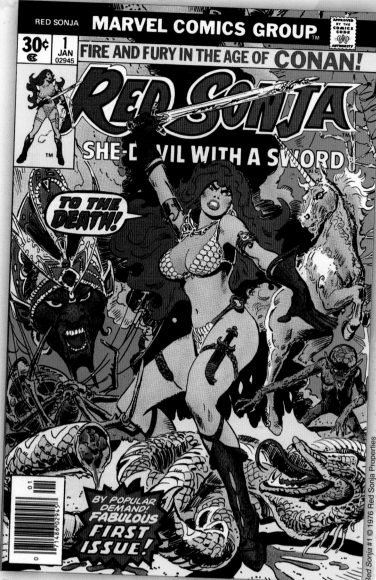

Red Sonja #1 (Nov 76)

Art by Frank Thorne

After her introduction in *Conan the Barbarian* #24 (Mar 73) with Barry Windsor-Smith dressing her in a chain-mail tunic and red shorts, it was up to artist Frank Thorne to provide Sonja's definitive look. It may appear to many to be an impractical outfit for adventuring, but it launched dozens of chain-mail bikinis at convention cosplay.

The Spirit #22 (Aug 50)

Art by Will Eisner

Will Eisner combined elements of sex and danger on this memorable, albeit final, cover of Quality's *Spirit* series.

> **The Spirit #22:** This Will Eisner cover is so powerful, the title character need not even appear!
>
> — *Jack Abramowitz*
> *CBG #1664, April 2010*

For more than half a century, Peter Parker has been wall-crawling and web-slinging his way across the Marvel Universe. Many Marvel heroes have had their ups and downs. But Peter Parker may be the champ of life-changing turmoil in the Marvel Universe. (And that's even if you discount the perpetually life-threatening crises of his Aunt May.)

Amazing Spider-Man #39 (Aug 66)
Art by John Romita

The Green Goblin had been a thorn in Spider-Man's side for a few years. The cover made it clear that the issue's revelations would take that conflict to a new level.

Amazing Spider-Man #33 (Feb 66)
Art by Steve Ditko

Ask almost any longtime Spider-Man fan to cite his or her favorite cover or story, and the answer will be, "The Final Chapter," in which Peter Parker realized once and for all the great responsibility he'd been handed. Steve Ditko's cover clearly conveys the heroic struggle.

Amazing Spider-Man #50 (Jul 67)
Art by John Romita

Many fans think an interior splash page of Peter Parker walking away from a trash can containing his Spider-Man suit was the issue's cover. Clearly, it wasn't the case — but the true cover demonstrated the same development in a different way.

Amazing Spider-Man #252 (May 84)
Art by Ron Frenz and Klaus Janson

No, Peter Parker wasn't replaced, but he updated his costume after nearly a quarter of a century. (Psst! This is also an homage cover, a tribute to Spidey's very first cover image.)

Spider-Man #1 (Aug 90)
Art by Todd McFarlane

The first issue of what is referred to by many as "adjectiveless" *Spider-Man* had a multitude of variants with both polybagged and non-polybagged editions.

Amazing Spider-Man #641 (Oct 10)
Art by Paolo Rivera

Artist Paolo Rivera's use of negative space emphasized the closeness of Peter and Mary Jane's relationship. What's important is neither words nor icons: It is two tormented, caring people alone in the world.

> *Amazing Spider-Man* #39: John Romita couldn't have drawn a more compelling image for his first Spidey issue.
> — *Craig "Mr. Silver Age" Shutt*
> *CBG* #1603, April 2005

The term was coined as a term to describe fans of Marvel Comics who mindlessly bought every comic book published by Marvel, no matter what. But "Marvel Zombies" takes on a whole new meaning, when you look at its horror output from the early 1950s (when it was known as Atlas).

Crazy #4 (Mar 54)
Art by Joe Maneely

Even Marvel's humor magazines had a zombie tie-in. (And this must have been aimed at older readers. For those not familiar with mixed drinks, a zombie is a combination of fruit juices, rum, and brandy.)

Menace #5 (Jul 53)
Art by Bill Everett

What's buried in this issue? Maddening menace for sure! Ik! And did this particular zombie come from the sewer? Double ik! (By the way, the Comics Code referred to in that star (a) did not last long and (b) was not the Comics Code from later in the decade. No zombies in that Comics Code. None.

Menace #9 (Jan 54)
Art by Gene Colan

Decades before Robert Kirkman turned *The Walking Dead* into a successful ongoing series (and more than a decade before George Romero's walking dead classic), Marvel used that zombie descriptor.

Marvel Tales #114 (May 53)
Art by Bill Everett

Is it a variation on the radio play (and later movie and TV episode) "Sorry, Wrong Number"? In any case, phone systems clearly worked differently in the 1950s. But, hey, potential purchasers got a free story just by looking at the cover. 'Nuff said!

Uncanny Tales #16 (Jan 56)
Art by Sol Brodsky

Remember what we said about the Comics Code on page 34? This was one of Marvel's last zombie covers for almost 20 years; the later-1950s version forbade the use of vampires, werewolves, and, yes, zombies.

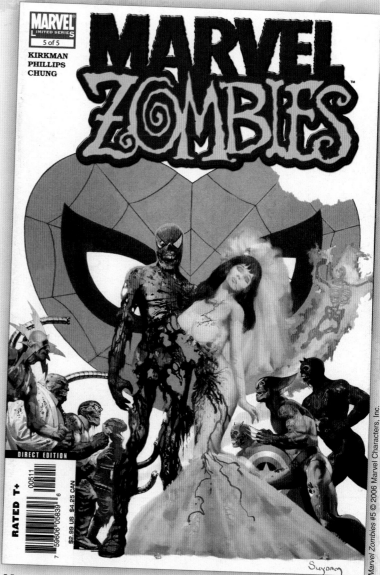

Marvel Zombies #5 (Jun 06)
Art by Arthur Suydam

But, after the beginning of the millennium, Marvel *embraced* its zombies, both the shambling kind and the fanboy kind, and saluted them with this first in a series of mini-series devoted to the walking dead. Arthur Suydam's horrific versions of earlier Marvel covers were the icing on the cake and captivated buyers in comics shops.

— *Ward Batty and Charlie Williams*
Trufan Adventures,
CBG #603, June 7, 1985

Following the introduction of super-heroes in The Golden Age and their reintroduction in The Silver Age, the next era of comics, which started in the early 1970s and ran to the mid-1980s, was The Bronze Age. The challenge for cover designers was to attract a new generation of readers.

Conan the Barbarian #1 (Oct 70)
Art by Barry Windsor-Smith and John Verpoorten

Barry Smith's version of Robert E. Howard's barbarian may have been powerful looking, but do you think his helm is a bit goofy? In any case, the issue captivated enough fans who usually limited collecting to costumed heroes — so the cover worked!

Superman #233 (Jan 71)
Art by Neal Adams

At this point in his career, Superman could move planets by listening hard. OK, that's an exaggeration, but his power levels were off the charts. Turning all the kryptonite on Earth to iron may have *appeared* to make Superman even more powerful (as shown with this Neal Adams cover), but the experiment that caused the change also temporarily weakened him. Obviously, any Superman fan had to grab the issue!

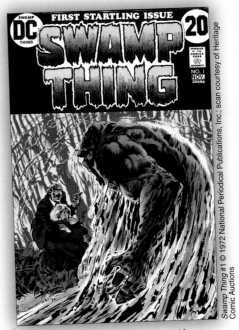

Swamp Thing #1 (Nov 72)
art by Bernie Wrightson

First introduced in a short story in *House of Secrets* #92 (Jul 71) by Len Wein (who referred to that story as "that swamp thing I'm working on") and Bernie Wrightson, DC's muck monster was both terrifying and soulful.

Marvel Spotlight #5 (Aug 72)
Art by Mike Ploog

A Comics Code revision allowed the return of such horror themes as vampires, werewolves, and zombies. Marvel could grab a character name from an earlier era and apply it to a skull-headed guy on a motorcycle. Buy it now!

Giant-Size X-Men #1 (Sum 75)
Art by Gil Kane and Dave Cockrum

After nearly half a decade as a reprint title, Marvel's X-Men returned to new adventures with this special issue. And whether it was the cover or the contents, readers quickly caught on that they'd better be grabbing an exciting series. Which is pretty much what the cover says, isn't it?

Incredible Hulk #181 (Nov 74)
Art by Herb Trimpe

OK, there's no way Wolverine on the cover was the sure-fire sales magnet at the time. It was his first full appearance, after all. But hey: Sales of the issue with this cover must have led to confidence in what was to come.

> ***Incredible Hulk #181:*** It's like a '67 Corvette Stingray racing toward a '66 Pontiac GTO — a collision course of two icons that will have resonance throughout the collective consciousness of generations of fans and creators for years to come.
>
> — *Mark Paniccia*
> *CBG #1639, March 2008*

Likenesses of presidents and other celebrities have appeared in comics and on their covers almost from the beginning. Why? For one thing, such guest-stars are sure to grab the buyer's attention, even if that buyer hasn't been buying the series. (These are single appearances. We eliminated licensed series featuring such ongoing characters as Bob Hope, Jerry Lewis, and Pat Boone.)

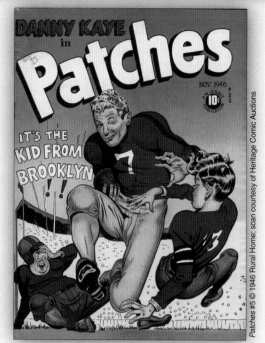

Patches #5 (Nov 46)
Art by L.B. Cole

This series featured a different celebrity guest each issue. Danny Kaye's radio show was in the midst of its run at the time and his latest film, *The Kid from Brooklyn*, had just been released, making him an ideal cover candidate.

Action Comics #127 (Dec 48)
Art by Al Plastino

Ralph Edwards put Superman through antics for a good cause and made for an intriguing cover. (Why was Superman in an apron, anyway?) The Man of Steel couldn't have appeared on Edwards' later program *This is Your Life*, since he would have seen through the set-up.

Marvel Team-Up #74 (Oct 78)
Art by Dave Cockrum and Marie Severin

Saturday Night Live was a hit and its characters household names to the demographic comics-buying audience. A team-up with Spider-Man was sure to sell.

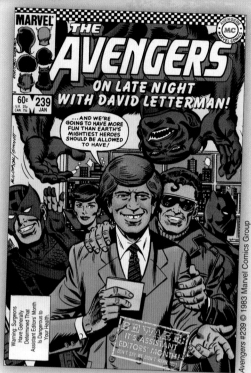

Avengers #239 (Jan 84)
Art by Al Milgrom and Joe Sinnott

Did Letterman's Top 10 list for this issue
come from the Avengers Mansion home
office? And what wackiness had the assistant
editor come up with?

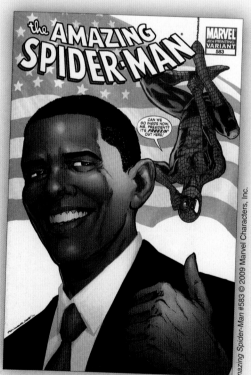

Amazing Spider-Man #583 (Mar 09)
Art by Phil Jimenez

President Obama's cover appearance pushed
this issue to multiple printings and five
variant covers. Collect them *all!*

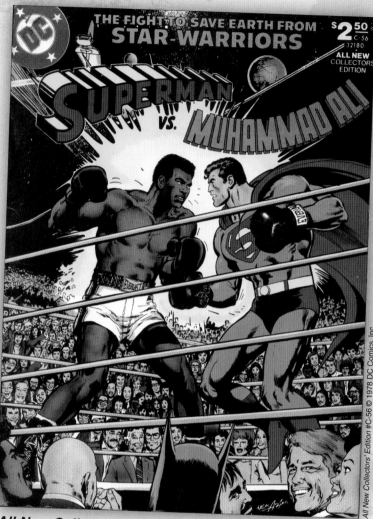

All New Collectors' Edition #C-56 (1978)
Art by Neal Adams

How could you have a Greatest Covers book without an appearance by
"The Greatest," Muhammad Ali? Artist Neal Adams not only captured
the champion in his prime, but also rendered dozens of celebrities
on both the front and back cover of this oversized one-shot. A key to
identifying them was provided inside. (If you find Waldo, you're one up
on us.)

> ***All New Collectors' Edition* #C-56:** I
> proclaimed to Neal Adams that I would
> like to recreate this image with all the
> relevant likenesses and background
> details, but legally, it would never be
> allowed.
>
> — *Alex Ross*
> *CBG #1621, October 2006*

Woo hoo! Here he comes! Here *they* come! They won't let brick walls or a circus hoop stand in their way — so they sure won't let the paper stock on the issue's cover keep them from leaping right out at you! Wow, they are eager! And *tough*! (And, yes, *Giant-Size X-Men* #1 could be included in this group, but remember we just used it on Page 37.)

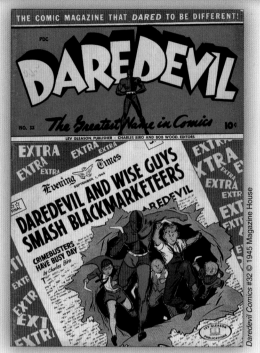

Daredevil Comics #32 (Sep 45)
Art by Charles Biro

Boomerangs at the ready, Daredevil and his gang of kid sidekicks blazed their way through a headline of their latest adventure. Could you wait to see what's inside? (Don't stop to over-analyze that newspaper: "Crimebusters have busy day"? Goodness.)

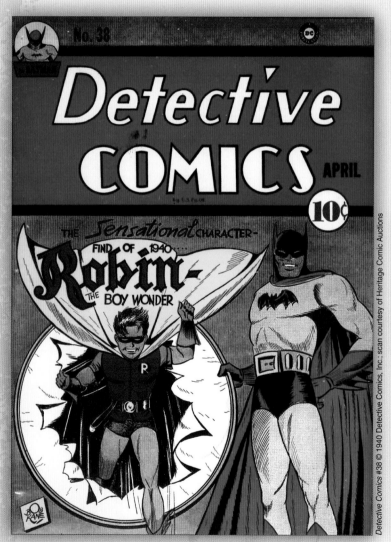

Detective Comics #38 (Apr 40)
Art by Bob Kane and Jerry Robinson

Robin burst onto the scene as one of the first costumed-hero sidekicks. And he immediately took on the vital role of giving the hero someone to talk to besides himself. Hi, there!

Flash Comics #26 (Feb 42)
Art by E.E. Hibbard

Is The Flash running on clouds — or is that the dust of his swift passage? It's clear who's starring in the issue, in any case (and *Flash Comics* was an anthology title, so it wasn't necessarily a given).

Captain America #109 (Jan 69)
Art by Jack Kirby and Syd Shores

With his re-introduction to the Marvel Universe, it was time to revisit Cap's origin — and fans love origin stories, whether or not a newspaper would have featured it on a front page in Marvel's New York City.

Fantastic Four #274 (Jan 85)
Art by John Byrne

At last! And, unlike so many of his fellow super-heroes, Ben Grimm crashed through something tougher than paper.

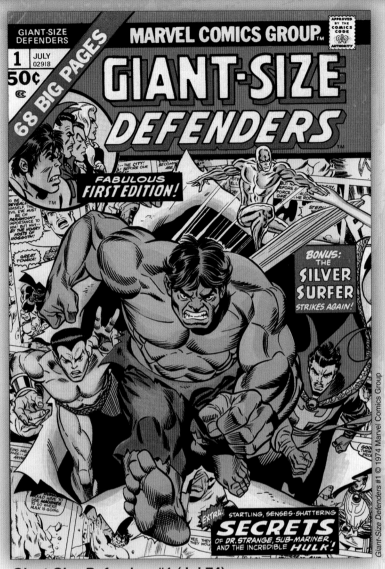

Giant-Size Defenders #1 (Jul 74)
Art by Gil Kane, John Romita, Frank Giacoia, and Mike Esposito

Almost a year before *Giant-Size X-Men* #1, Gil Kane had a similar cover design for The Defenders' first giant-size issue. (Yes, we told you once but now maybe you'd like to compare the images. It's on page 37.) No reason to avoid using the idea twice, right?

> **Giant-Size Defenders #1:** One of the all-time great team-book compositions, this time with our Jolly Jade Giant leading the way and breaking the fourth wall.
>
> — *Mark Paniccia*
> *CBG #1639, March 2008*

During World War II, comics creators had a challenge besides paper shortages. It was the intersection of the realities of the battlefield and the fantasies of super-heroes. There were tales of combat, but often the focus had to be adapted, as the war effort continued. Airboy and Captain America tackled Nazis, to be sure, but it was *after* the war that the war genre exploded with exciting, heroic tales of fighting forces. (While some were realistic, many were designed solely to entertain and some were downright silly.)

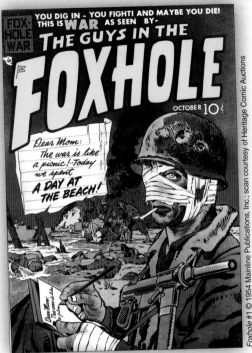

Foxhole #1 (Sep 54)
Art by Jack Kirby

Artist Jack Kirby saw some of the worst that World War II had to offer in the European theater and brought those memories to his post-war work.

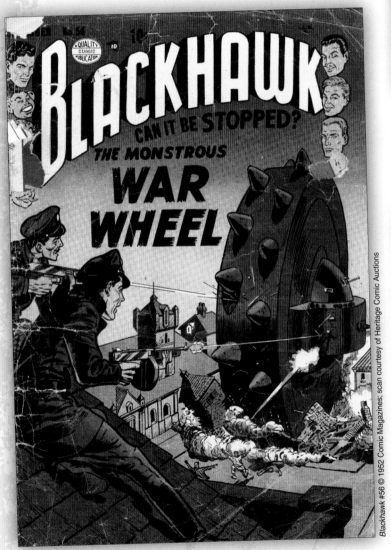

Blackhawk #56 (Sep 52)
Art by Reed Crandall

The Blackhawk Squadron, an international team of fighting aviators, actually began their adventures before America entered World War II. Eventually, they took on all sorts of menaces in a decades-long version of that conflict. The War Wheel was such a weird and memorable adversary that it returned several times after its debut in this issue.

Star Spangled War Stories #90 (May 60)
Art by Ross Andru and Mike Esposito

"The War That Time Forgot" was an ongoing theme in DC's war titles. The science may have been way off, but the action was worth it. How could a story go wrong with tanks *and* dinosaurs?

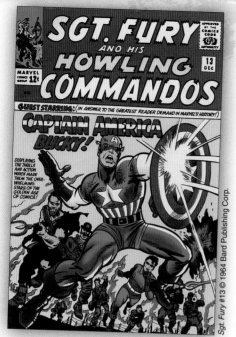

Sgt. Fury #13 (Dec 64)
Art by Jack Kirby

Teaming a revived Captain America with Sgt. Fury was a logical move for Marvel nearly two decades after the armed conflict ended. (Historical postscript: When the first proposed cover for this issue was rejected, the artist drew expletives on Cap's shield on the original art.)

Warfront #37 (Sep 66)
Art by Jack Sparling and Wally Wood

Readers of war comics have seen all sorts of weaponry — from grenades disabling tanks to machine guns taking out dinosaurs — but how about a Marine using sticks of dynamite as a weapon of choice? He was clearly blast-crazy!

Sgt. Rock #408 (Sep 86)
Art by Joe Kubert

Under the hand of editor-writer-artist Joe Kubert, DC's war titles showed the grittier side of war and urged readers, at one point, to "Make War No More." This unusual issue's stunning cover paid tribute to those sentiments while also celebrating the career of DC's Sheldon Mayer.

Foxhole #1: This is probably my favorite cover of all time. To me, Kirby's amazing illustration here stands head and shoulders above his more fantastic "super-hero" art.

— *Billy Tucci*
CBG #1648, December 2008

The Bronze Age (see Page 36) hadn't yet ended in the early 1980s, when these issues were published. Even so, these were years in which storytelling changes began that still resonate today. [Psst! There's still heated debate — not only about when the Bronze Age ended, but also about what to call the *next* Age (or Ages) and when it (or they) began.]

X-Men #141 (Jan 81)
Art by John Byrne and Terry Austin

Not content to maintain the status quo, writer Chris Claremont provided readers a peek at a possible future for Marvel's mutants. John Byrne and Terry Austin's cover made clear the impact of the apocalyptic tale.

New Teen Titans #1 (Nov 80)
Art by George Pérez

DC provided its answer to Marvel's revived X-Men with Marv Wolfman and George Pérez' reimagining of DC's junior Justice League as a team that could hold its own against its older counterparts. That team is comin' atcha! (And, yes, it *was* a "collector's item issue"!)

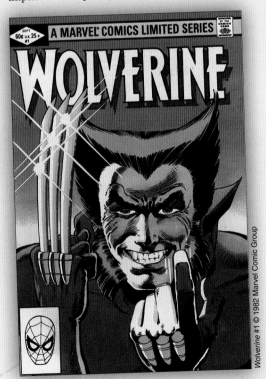

Wolverine (1st series) #1 (Sep 82)
Art by Frank Miller

Logan has always had a bad attitude, but Frank Miller brought it to the fore in the Canadian mutant's first solo mini-series. Come on! Buy it! You *know* you want to!

Thor #337 (Nov 83)
Art by Walt Simonson

Alien Beta Ray Bill showed he was worthy of Thor's hammer with this powerful Walter Simonson cover.

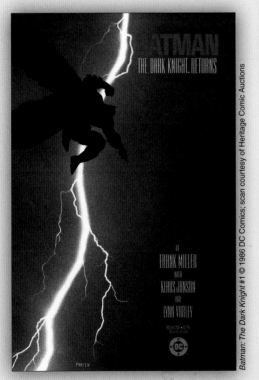

Batman: The Dark Knight #1 (Mar 86)
Art by Frank Miller and Lynn Varley

It may say "Returns" on the cover, but the indicia doesn't contain the word. The cover was so iconic, many other artists have drawn homages to it.

Watchmen #1 (Sep 86)
Art by Dave Gibbons

Dave Gibbons' powerful first cover for his and Alan Moore's genre-defining maxi-series turned a familiar popular-culture icon of joy into a symbol of darkness. (The Gibbons image has itself become an icon of social comment.)

Thor #337: Man, oh man, who wouldn't want to know who this guy is after seeing this cover?

— *Robert Kirkman*
CBG #1642, June 2008

I n E.C. Segar's *Thimble Theatre* comic strip in the 1930s the J. Wellington Wimpy character sometimes managed to avoid being personally injured by suggesting, "Let's you and him fight," when fisticuffs were in the offing. None of the battles on these covers were sparked by that phrase, but they deserve comparison to the best of the spinach-fueled encounters that Wimpy's buddy Popeye experienced.

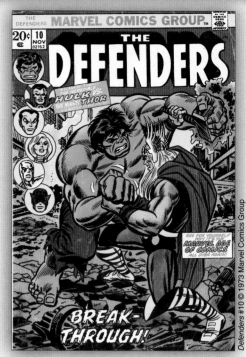

Defenders #10 (Nov 73)
Art by John Romita

Fans have argued for years about the question: Who's stronger, The Hulk or Thor? Unfortunately, the matter wasn't actually settled in the issue — though the cover successfully tantalized readers.

Marvel Mystery Comics #9 (Jul 40)
Art by Bill Everett and Alex Schomburg

Two of the titans of Marvel Comics' predecessor, Timely Comics, came to blows repeatedly in the 1940s, making for spectacular donnybrooks. This example is actually a bit restrained for an Alex Schomburg cover; the artist specialized in packing his images with a plethora of background details.

X-Men #100 (Aug 76)
Art by Dave Cockrum

"Let's you and him fight" is often epitomized by a face-off between two teams — or generations — of heroes. The artist presents an exciting view of the possibilities ahead.

Justice League of America #137 (Dec 83)

Art by Ernie Chua

Who *cared* how red kryptonite ended up at The Rock of Eternity? This was the battle for which fans had asked for more than 40 years! Woo hoo!

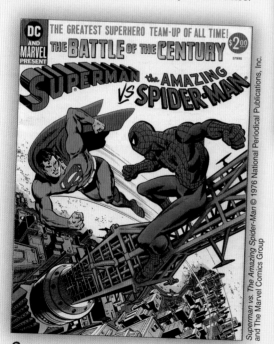

Superman vs. The Amazing Spider-Man (1976)

Art by Carmine Infantino, Ross Andru, Neal Adams, Dick Giordano, and Terry Austin

Pitting their most popular characters against each other was a natural sales blockbuster for DC and Marvel. Talk about fan debates comparing super-heroes!

Avengers/JLA #2 (2003)

Art by George Pérez

An earlier version of this crossover between Marvel and DC had been planned nearly 20 years previously. Fans rejoiced when the patience of artist George Pérez was rewarded when he was finally able to realize his vision with writer Kurt Busiek. It was hero vs. hero vs. hero vs. ... Well, you get the idea.

> **Superman vs. The Amazing Spider-Man:** Or as I like to call it: The invention of the nerdgasm.
>
> — **Brian Michael Bendis CBG #1613, February 2006**

Robert Louis Stevenson's *Strange Case of Dr. Jekyll and Mr. Hyde* has inspired countless variations on the theme since 1896. Stan Lee and Jack Kirby came up with a comics version in 1962, and, in the last half-century, numerous writers and artists have added variations to the basics. The primal nature of the character and his powerful covers have appealed to fans for 50 years.

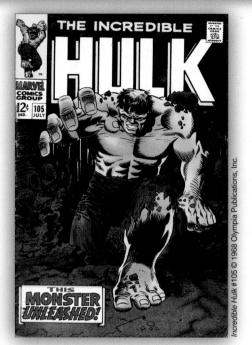

Incredible Hulk #105 (Jul 68)
Art by Marie Severin and Frank Giacoia

He was powerful. Heck, he was incredible! And artist Marie Severin made The Hulk's power clear in this early issue of his ongoing run. (The series picked up the numbering of Marvel's *Tales to Astonish*.)

Incredible Hulk King-Size Special #1 (1968)
Art by Jim Steranko and Marie Severin

Artist Jim Steranko captured the power of The Hulk with Ol' Greenskin's own logo demonstrating his strength. Marie Severin redrew The Hulk's face for this memorable image.

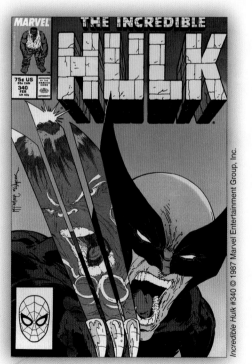

Incredible Hulk #340 (Feb 88)
Art by Todd McFarlane

The green Hulk had taken a breather, so it was up to the less-powerful (but more cunning) gray version of The Hulk to battle Wolverine. (The cover was so dynamic that it was later used in a poster with green Hulk in place of gray.)

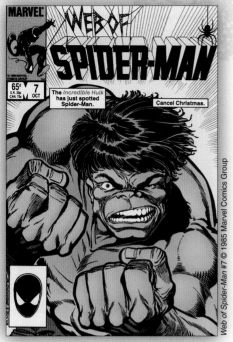

Web of Spider-Man #7 (Oct 85)
Art by Ron Wilson and Brett Breeding

Readers were invited to imagine how it would feel to face a fighting-mad Hulk. You have to figure it's something any sane Wall-Crawler would want to avoid.

Incredible Hulk #376 (Dec 90)
Art by Dale Keown and Bob McLeod

Green vs. Gray was the order of the day, as writer Peter David and artist Dale Keown integrated all aspects of The Hulk and his alter-ego Bruce Banner. Clearly, it was a must-buy issue!

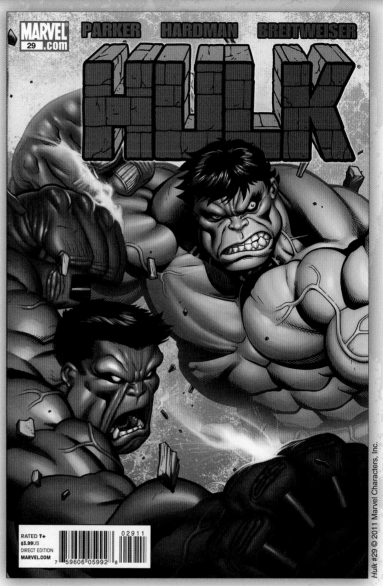

Hulk #29 (Mar 11)
Art by Ed McGuinness

As if green and gray Hulks weren't enough, how about a *red* Hulk? Maybe this cover should have been in our "Let's You and Him Fight" section.

Incredible Hulk King-Size Special #1: The still pose exudes momentum, as Hulk struggles to keep the weight of the world on his shoulders.

— *Mark Paniccia*
CBG #1639, March 2008

Science-fiction stories were a natural fit for comics. After all, most of the super-hero adventures were science fiction to some extent. From space adventures that began in the pulps and newspapers to cosmic adventures to tales set a long time ago in a galaxy far, far away or out where no man has gone before, such comics can be stellar. (Moreover, even spectacular special effects are cheap in comics.)

Famous Funnies #213 (Sep 54)
Art by Frank Frazetta

Frank Frazetta added excitement to reprints of the long-running *Buck Rogers* newspaper stories with his memorable covers of the mid-1950s. Who — or what — is that shadowy figure menacing Buck and Wilma?

Flying Saucers #1 (1950)
Art by Gene Fawcette

First coined in the late 1940s, the term "flying saucers" quickly conjured the image of aliens (sometimes "little green men") bent on invasion. Avon Publications tapped into paranoia with this 1950 one-shot and its provocative cover question. Oooo! What did Professor Lanning know? Find out for a dime!

Mystery in Space #53 (Aug 59)
Art by Gil Kane and Bernard Sachs

Adam Strange was a man of two worlds. While his archaeological expeditions on Earth were exciting, it was his galactic gallivanting on Rann that made him a hero to an entire world. Doggone those revolting robots, anyway!

Silver Surfer #1 (Aug 68)
Art by John Buscema and Joe Sinnott

Readers had already met the tragic interstellar character who had come as an enemy and remained as an ally. But they hadn't been told the full tale of his origin — so this was a natural hook to catch Faithful Fans of The Fantastic Four.

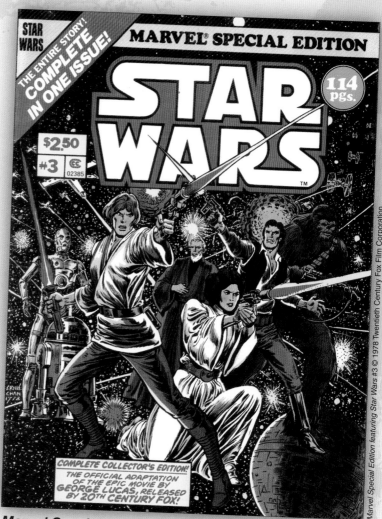

Marvel Special Edition featuring Star Wars #3 (1978)

Fans of the first *Star Wars* film (now known as *Star Wars Episode IV: A New Hope*) had multiple comic-book options to read the adaptation. There were the first six issues of the ongoing comic book, two *Life* magazine-sized volumes with the same material, and this single oversized volume, which collected the whole story and featured the most dynamic cover of all the versions.

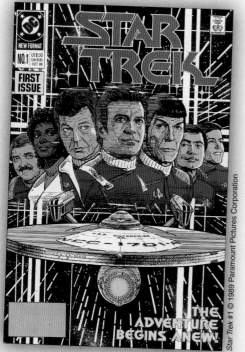

Star Trek #1 (Oct 89)
Art by Jerome Moore

All the major players of the original series were recognizable on the cover of the first issue of DC's second series: a must-buy for fans who wanted to move past the events of *Star Trek V: The Undiscovered Country.*

> *Marvel Special Edition featuring Star Wars #3:* George Lucas' characters and Marvel were a successful match.
>
> — *Tony Isabella*
> *1000 Comic Books You Must Read, 2009*

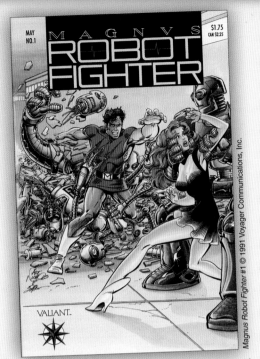

The 1990s ushered in an era of new publishers, new printing techniques, and a variety of cover effects (as well as a speculation bubble that burst mid-decade). The principles designed to attract readers were not forgotten, however, as these memorable covers demonstrate.

Magnus Robot Fighter #1 (May 91)
Art by Art Nichols and Bob Layton

With its acquisition of a license to publish new adventures of Gold Key's heroes of the 1960s, Valiant set the bar high with its first issue of *Magnus Robot Fighter*. It was designed to grab new readers as well as fans of the earlier series.

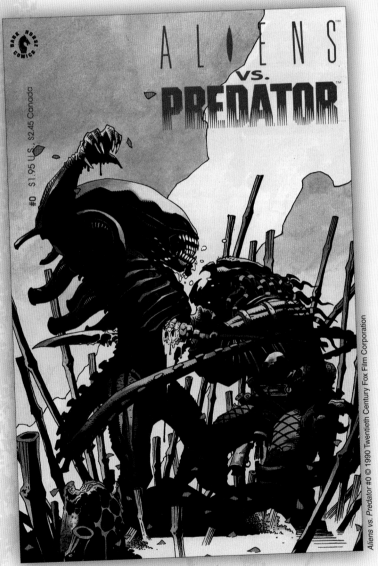

Aliens vs. Predator #0 (Jul 90)
Art by Mike Mignola

With the licenses for both properties, Dark Horse Comics merged two popular movie franchises years before the studios did so. It was a "must-buy" for any fan of either — as this cover made clear! (And — hey — which would *you* root for?)

Bone #3 (Dec 91)
Art by Jeff Smith

The manipulative schemer Phoney Bone couldn't help but meddle in his cousin Fone Bone's affairs, even usurping the cover of an early issue. The cover was an attention-grabber for a series destined to be recognized as a classic.

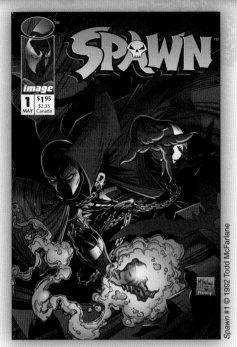

Spawn #1 © 1992 Todd McFarlane

Spawn #1 (May 92)
Art by Todd McFarlane

Todd McFarlane's Hell-born hero was an
early title from Image. Its dynamic art
captivated buyers from the very first issue
and spawned (sorry!) an animated series,
live-action feature, videogames, collectible
action figures, and more.

Preacher #1 © 1995 Garth Ennis and Steve Dillon

Preacher #1 (Apr 95)
Art by Steve Dillon

Artist Steve Dillon began his and Garth
Ennis' metaphysical adventure series with
this compelling image.

Marvels #1 © 1993 Marvel Entertainment Group, Inc.

Marvels #1 (Jan 94)
Art by Alex Ross

Alex Ross' re-imagining of The Human Torch's first appearance in 1939
set the tone for this mini-series. Writer Kurt Busiek and artist Ross
worked together to tell the history of the Marvel Universe from the view
of news photographer Phil Sheldon. The unusual cover featured an
overlay carrying the text so that the art could be viewed on its own.

> **Spawn #1:** I can't deny that this was one
> of the most influential titles on me when
> it debuted in '92. I was about 15 and
> blown away by the art.
>
> — *Josh Blaylock*
> *CBG #1616, May 2006*

The cover of *Crisis on Infinite Earths* #7 may be the most memorable version of covers that are based in part on Michaelangelo's Pietà, but it wasn't the first comics cover to feature a dead character in someone's arms while other characters looked on.

Thor #127 (Apr 66)
Art by Jack Kirby

Sure looks as though Thor has gone to Valhalla, doesn't it? What does Odin have to say about it? Better buy that issue!

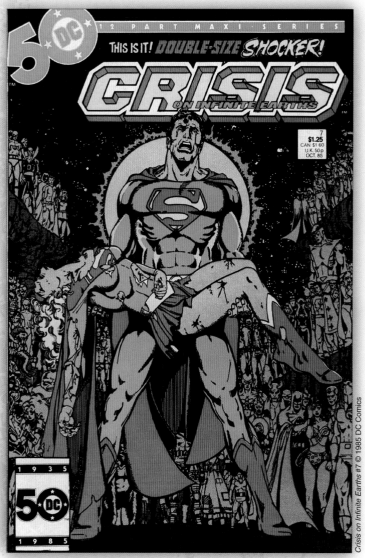

Crisis on Infinite Earths #7 (Oct 85)
Art by George Pérez

George Pérez' art showed clearly that *no* character was safe, as DC overhauled and simplified its universe after 50 years. But how did Supergirl — whose powers were nearly as infinite as her cousin's — die? *That's* what readers *had* to find out in this double-sized issue.

Superman's Girl Friend Lois Lane #128 (Dec 72)
Art by Bob Oksner

Superman just can't catch a break. Every time he thinks he's found happiness with Lois, something comes along to mess it up. What now? Hey, just buy the issue, already.

Incredible Hulk #189 © 1975 Marvel Comics Group

Incredible Hulk #189 (Jul 75)
Art by Herb Trimpe

Ol' Jade Jaws spends less time mourning and more time taking action, when his friend is injured. Fewer tears, more sheer rage. Can The Mole Man and his Moloids help? Holy Moly!

X-Men #136 © 1980 Marvel Comics Group

X-Men #136 (Aug 80)
Art by John Byrne and Terry Austin

It was another major turning point. This was clearly a can't-miss-it issue. X-Men fans *had* to see what had happened to Jean Grey!

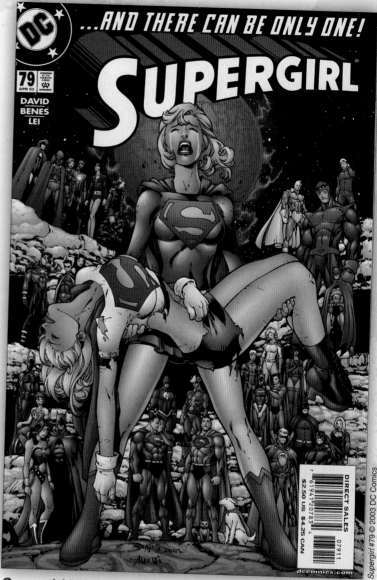

Supergirl #79 © 2003 DC Comics

Supergirl #79 (Apr 03)
Art by Ed Benes and Alex Lei

Wait a minute! What the heck? Didn't we *just* see *Crisis on Infinite Earths* #7? Writer Peter David and artists Ed Benes and Alex Lei played with that issue's events — and cover — in this story.

> ***Crisis on Infinite Earths* #7:** An anguished Superman holds the body of Kara after she's been killed. That cover made the whole comics world reassess their opinion of Supergirl.
>
> — Kevin J. Anderson
> CBG #1641, May 2008

Reinvention, relaunches, and revamps were the order of the day in the new millennium's first decade. Shaking up the status quo was designed to increase readership. Fresh, exciting covers and concepts didn't hurt, either — and some attracted mass-media attention.

JLA #41 (May 00)
Art by Howard Porter and John Dell

While working with a core group of major characters, writer Grant Morrison didn't have to limit his version of The Justice League to any particular size. This cover made the concept clear, even to the casual reader.

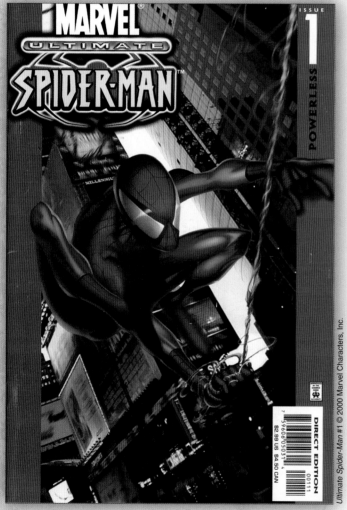

Ultimate Spider-Man #1 (Oct 00)
Art by Mark Bagley

Writer Brian Michael Bendis and artist Mark Bagley reimagined Spider-Man as a teenager in a separate, modern Marvel Universe. Updated versions of other characters from the original Marvel Universe were also reintroduced in a plan that gave Marvel double sales for its trademarked icons. (Note the trade dress [see page 4] designed to distinguish this series from stories in the *other* Spider-Man's universe.)

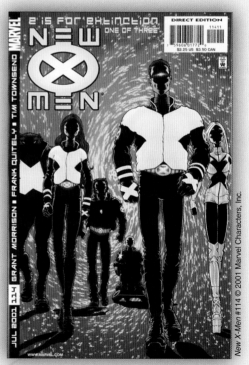

New X-Men #114 (Jul 01)
Art by Frank Quitely and Tim Townsend

Grant Morrison and Frank Quitely used what was meant as a joke in the first *X-Men* film when they took a turn at *X-Men (2nd series)*, renaming their run as *New X-Men*. (The move still drives indexers crazy. Striking cover, though!)

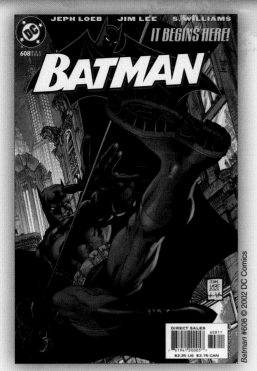

Batman #608 (Dec 02)

Art by Jim Lee

New revelations about Batman's past were revealed in the "Hush" story arc, along with revisions to his costume, the Batmobile, and several villains. It certainly *did* begin here — as the cover boasted!

The Walking Dead #1 (Oct 03)

Art by Tony Moore

Robert Kirkman's long-running zombie series began with Tony Moore's cover, which revealed more upon reflection.

Archie #600 (Oct 09)

Art by Stan Goldberg and Bob Smith

After nearly 70 years of wondering which girl Archie would choose to marry, fans appeared to get the answer. However, it turned out to illustrate an imaginary story which showed two *possible* futures: one in which Archie married Veronica and the other in which he and Betty tied the knot. Fan response led to an ongoing magazine which continues to explore the two different possibilities.

New X-Men #114: Like many fanboys, I've sworn never to pick up another copy of X-Men in my life. And, like a gambling addict in Vegas, I always go back to the table. Grant Morrison's run on the title was the first time I got sucked back in.

— Christopher Farnsworth
CBG #1681, September 2011

D o you spot Stan Lee when he appears in Marvel movies? It's not only on film that he and other creators have appeared over the years. Some have even made the cover!

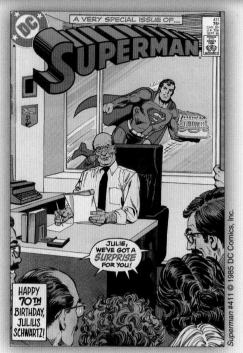

Superman #411 (Sep 85)
Art uncredited

After he'd served more than a decade as editor of the Superman titles (and almost 40 years at DC), a special issue of *Superman* was produced featuring Julius Schwartz. It was another fan-directed attraction.

What If? #11 (Oct 78)
Art by Jack Kirby and Joe Sinnott

Writer and editor Stan Lee as Mr. Fantastic, artist Jack Kirby as The Thing, production manager Sol Brodsky as The Human Torch, and secretary "Fabulous" Flo Steinberg as The Invisible Woman made for a fabulous foursome cameo. It was clearly designed to be a "must-buy" for Faithful Fans.

> **What If? #11:** Who could resist this one?
> — *Bob Almond*
> *CBG #1626, March 2007*

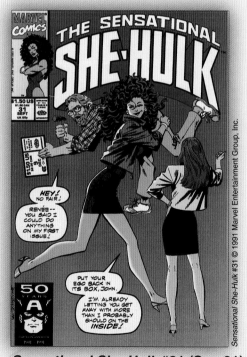

Sensational She-Hulk #31 (Sep 91)
Art by John Byrne

Writer-artist John Byrne inserted himself into several titles on which he worked. In *Sensational She-Hulk*, it became a running gag, as the series regularly broke the "fourth wall": an approach designed to catch the eye and grab the buyer.

TOP 10 FAVORITE COMIC BOOK COVERS

CHOSEN BY DIVERSE HANDS

Part of the inspiration for this book was the monthly *Top 10 Favorite Comic Book Covers* in our **Comics Buyer's Guide**, the longest-running U.S. magazine about comics. Since 2005, we've asked industry professionals, **CBG** contributors, novelists, and fans, among others, to tell us what their 10 favorites are. Some have sent in themed lists, many have contributed bizarre choices, but *all* responses have been interesting and informative and, with more than 900 comics chosen, an incredible variety was *someone's* favorite. An index of all the Top 10 lists through early 2012 revealed these comics as the top picks.

10.

X-Men #1 © 1963 Canam Publishers Sales Corp.

X-Men #1 (Sep 63)
Art by Jack Kirby

Marvel's mutants and The Avengers arrived almost simultaneously, giving fans of the day quite a choice of teams. Jack Kirby provided the art for both covers, so that probably didn't aid the decision-making. In this case, though, Kirby had to make clear some of this new group's powers.

9.

Superman vs. The Amazing Spider-Man © 1976 National Periodical Publications, Inc. and The Marvel Comics Group

Superman vs. The Amazing Spider-Man (1976)
Art by Carmine Infantino, Ross Andru, Neal Adams, Dick Giordano, and Terry Austin

The goal was to provide an unforgettable image, as the two giants of the industry produced their first official crossover. Mission accomplished!

8.

Nick Fury, Agent of S.H.I.E.L.D. #4 (Sep 68)
Art by Jim Steranko

While the 1960s influences are evident in Jim Steranko's design, his imaginative covers still resonate with fans today.

7.

Mystery in Space #90 (Mar 64)
Art by Carmine Infantino and Murphy Anderson

Carmine Infantino and Murphy Anderson created stunning space sequences for the Adam Strange stories, and this is the one that stuck with the most "Top 10" contributors.

6.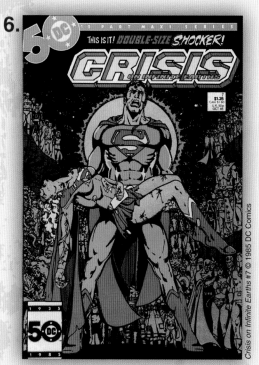

Crisis on Infinite Earths #7 (Oct 85)
Art by George Pérez

As shown on Page 54, it wasn't the first cover to feature this particular composition, but George Pérez' presentation is the one more fans remember. Moreover, it marked an unexpected turning point in DC continuity at the time.

5.

Amazing Spider-Man #28 (Sep 65)
Art by Steve Ditko

You saw the technique on page 33, and here's *another* cover that utilized negative space to highlight the characters. It's a stunner (even though its solid blacks make it almost impossible to find it in top grades as a back issue).

4.

Amazing Spider-Man #50 © 1967 Non-Pareil Publishing Corp.; scan courtesy of Heritage Comic Auctions

Amazing Spider-Man #50 (Jul 67)
Art by John Romita

This issue featured *two* memorable images: this cover and the interior splash page that featured Peter Parker walking away from a trash can in which he'd dumped his costume. (Some even mistakenly recall that splash page as being the cover.)

3.

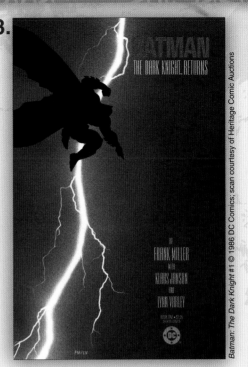

Batman: The Dark Knight #1 © 1986 DC Comics; scan courtesy of Heritage Comic Auctions

Batman: The Dark Knight #1 (Mar 86)
Art by Frank Miller and Lynn Varley

The iconic (and often imitated) look of this cover made it a natural choice for many. Though occasionally credited by some to Frank Miller alone, it was Lynn Varley's colors that helped make the image pop.

2.

Thor #337 © 1983 Marvel Entertainment Group, Inc.

Thor #337 (Nov 83)
Art by Walt Simonson

Beta Ray Bill's assumption of Thor's role was memorable, not only for the changes it brought to the title, but also for Walter Simonson's powerful cover.

1.

Avengers #4 © 1963 Vista Publications, Inc.; scan courtesy of Heritage Comic Auctions

Avengers #4 (Mar 64)
Art by Jack Kirby

Is it any surprise that so many fans *and professionals* fondly remember Jack Kirby's re-introduction of Captain America to the Marvel Universe? Any Marvel fan who saw this image on the newsstand in 1964 *had* to buy the issue!

A nd now, the time has come ...

Marvel Family #89 (Jun 54)
Art by Kurt Schaffenberger

It's more than a little ironic that *Marvel Family*'s final issue featured a story in which the characters disappeared. Yikes!

Savage She-Hulk #25 (Feb 82)
Art by Mike Vosburg and Terry Austin

It may be as clichéd as "She-Hulk's Back!" — but this final-issue cover of Shulkie's first series was memorable. Yes, even with a bike ad distracting from its impact.

Action Comics #583 (Sep 86)
Art by Curt Swan, Murphy Anderson, and Ed Hannigan

Writer Alan Moore and longtime Superman artists Curt Swan, Kurt Schaffenberger, and Murphy Anderson gave Superman a fitting send-off before The Man of Steel was revamped by writer and artist John Byrne. It was clearly designed to grab anyone who'd ever loved The Man of Steel.

ARTISTS

Many fine artists from the 1930s to today have provided the striking images chosen for this book. We thank them for their memorable work.

Neal Adams *Action Comics #399, All New Collectors' Edition #C-56, Green Lantern (2nd series) #76, Superman #233, Superman vs. The Amazing Spider-Man*
Murphy Anderson *Action Comics #583, Brave and the Bold #28, Flash #123, Green Lantern (2nd series) #40, Mystery in Space #90*
Ross Andru *Flash #186, Star Spangled War Stories #90, Superman vs. The Amazing Spider-Man*
Terry Austin *Savage She-Hulk #25, Superman vs. The Amazing Spider-Man, Uncanny X-Men #142, X-Men #136, X-Men #141*
Dick Ayers *Tense Suspense #1*
Mark Bagley *Ultimate Spider-Man #1*
Bernard Baily *Mister Mystery #12, More Fun Comics #65*
Matt Baker *Phantom Lady #17*
Darryl Banks *Green Lantern #49*
Carl Barks *Four Color Comics #199, Four Color Comics #223*
John Beatty *Captain America #284*
C.C. Beck *Captain Marvel Adventures #16, Captain Marvel Adventures #97, Marvel Family #7*
Ed Benes *Supergirl #79*
Jack Binder *Mary Marvel #5*
Charles Biro *Daredevil Comics #32*
Jon Bogdanove *Superman: The Man of Steel #30*
Wayne Boring *Superman #32*
Pat Boyette *Charlton Premiere Vol. 2 #2*
Brett Breeding *Web of Spider-Man #7*
Sol Brodsky *Uncanny Tales #16*
Al Bryant *Doll Man Quarterly #6*
Carl Buettner *Walt Disney's Comics & Stories #22*
John Buscema *Fantastic Four #126, Silver Surfer #1*
Ernie Bushmiller *Sparkle Comics #3*
John Byrne *Avengers West Coast #54, Fantastic Four #274, Man of Steel #1, Marvel Age #14, Sensational She-Hulk #31, Superman & Batman: Generations #1, X-Men #136, X-Men #141, X-Men #142*
Nick Cardy *World's Finest Comics #221*
Ernie Chua *Justice League of America #137*
Dave Cockrum *Giant-Size X-Men #1, Marvel Special Edition featuring Star Wars #3, Marvel Team-Up #74, X-Men #100*
Gene Colan *Menace #9*
L.B. Cole *Patches #5*
Pete Costanza *Marvel Family #7*
Johnny Craig *Crime SuspenStories #22, Extra! #3*
Reed Crandall *Blackhawk #56*
Jack Davis *Tales from the Crypt #46*
John Dell *JLA #41*
Steve Dillon *Preacher #1*
Steve Ditko *Amazing Fantasy #15, Amazing Spider-Man #28, Amazing Spider-Man #33, Strange Suspense Stories #19*
Will Eisner *Spirit #22*
Mike Esposito *Flash #186, Giant-Size Defenders #1, Star Spangled War Stories #90*
Bill Everett *Marvel Mystery Comics #9, Marvel Tales #114, Menace #5*
Gene Fawcette *Flying Saucers #1*
Al Feldstein *Tales from the Crypt #28*
Frank Frazetta *Famous Funnies #213*
Ron Frenz *Amazing Spider-Man #252*
Dave Gibbons *Watchmen #1*
Frank Giacoia *Giant-Size Avengers #3, Giant-Size Defenders #1, Incredible Hulk #105*
Joe Giella *Flash #163, Green Lantern #5*
Dick Giordano *Superman vs. The Amazing Spider-Man*
Stan Goldberg *Archie #600*
Dan Green *Wolverine #50*
Ed Hannigan *Action Comics #583*
Irwin Hasen *All-Star Comics #37*
E.E. Hibbard *Flash Comics #26*
Rick Hoberg *Marvel Special Edition featuring Star Wars #3*
Carmine Infantino *All-American Comics #95, Flash #123, Flash #163, Mystery in Space #90, Showcase #4, Superman vs. The Amazing Spider-Man*
Klaus Janson *Amazing Spider-Man #252*
Phil Jimenez *Amazing Spider-Man #583*
Bob Kane *Detective Comics #27, Detective Comics #38*
Gil Kane *Giant-Size Avengers #3, Giant-Size Defenders #1, Giant-Size X-Men #1, Green Lantern (2nd series) #5, Green Lantern (2nd series) #40, Mystery in Space #53*
Jack Kamen *All Top Comics #10*
Stan Kaye *Adventure Comics #247, Superboy #47, Superman #149, Superman's Girl Friend Lois Lane #19*
Dale Keown *Incredible Hulk #376*
H.C. Kiefer *Stories by Famous Authors Illustrated #1*
Jack Kirby *Amazing Fantasy #15, Avengers #4, Captain America #109, Captain America Comics #1, Fantastic Four #1, Foxhole #1, Sgt. Fury #13, Thor #127, What If? #11, X-Men #1*
George Klein *Superman #156, World's Finest Comics #172*
Joe Kubert *Sgt. Rock #408, Showcase #4*
Harvey Kurtzman *Two-Fisted Tales #25*

Howard Larsen *Slave Girl Comics #1*
Bob Layton *Magnus Robot Fighter #1*
Jim Lee *Batman #608*
Alex Lei *Supergirl #79*
Dave Manak *ALF #48*
Joe Maneely *Crazy #4*
George Marcoux *Supersnipe Comics Vol. 1 #7*
Sheldon Mayer *Sugar & Spike #17*
Todd McFarlane *Incredible Hulk #340, Spawn #1, Spider-Man #1*
Ed McGuinness *Hulk #29*
Bob McLeod *Incredible Hulk #376*
Jesus Merino *Green Lantern (4th series) #1*
Mike Mignola *Aliens vs. Predator #0*
Al Milgrom *Avengers #239*
Frank Miller *Batman: The Dark Knight #1, Wolverine #1*
Jerome Moore *Star Trek #1*
Tony Moore *Walking Dead #1*
Rags Morales *Action Comics (2nd series) #1*
Bill Morrison *Simpsons Comics #1*
David Mowry *Married ... with Children: Quantum Quartet #1*
Art Nichols *Magnus Robot Fighter #1*
Bob Oksner *Superman's Girl Friend Lois Lane #128*
Jerry Ordway *Power of Shazam #1*
Fred Ottenheimer *Eh! #4*
Carlos Pacheco *Green Lantern (4th series) #1*
Frank R. Paul *Marvel Comics #1*
George Pérez *Avengers/JLA #2, Crisis on Infinite Earths #7, New Teen Titans #1*
Photo cover *Rifleman #10*
Al Plastino *Action Comics #127*
Mike Ploog *Marvel Spotlight #5*
Howard Porter *JLA #41*
Howard Purcell *Green Lantern (1st series) #1*
Frank Quitely *New X-Men #114*
Mac Raboy *America's Greatest Comics #1, Captain Marvel Jr. #21, Master Comics #32*
Fred Ray *Superman #14*
Tom Richmond *Married ... with Children: Quantum Quartet #1*
Paolo Rivera *Amazing Spider-Man #641*
Jerry Robinson *Detective Comics #38*
John Romita *Amazing Spider-Man #39, Amazing Spider-Man #50, Amazing Spider-Man #50, Defenders #10, Giant-Size Defenders #1*
Alex Ross *Marvels #1*
George Roussos *Avengers #4*
Bernard Sachs *Mystery in Space #53*
Kurt Schaffenberger *Marvel Family #89, Superman #162*
Alex Schomburg *Marvel Mystery Comics #9, Startling Comics #49*
Mike Sekowsky *Brave and the Bold #28*
Marie Severin *Incredible Hulk #105, Incredible Hulk Annual #1, Marvel Team-Up #74*
Syd Shores *Captain America #109*
Joe Shuster *Action Comics #1, Superman #1*
Marc Silvestri *Wolverine #50*
Joe Simon *Captain America Comics #1*
Walter Simonson *Thor #337, Thor #364*
Joe Sinnott *Avengers #239, Fantastic Four #126, Silver Surfer #1, What If? #11*
Bob Smith *Archie #600*
Jeff Smith *Bone #3*
Jack Sparling *Warfront #37*
Frank Springer *Secret Six #1*
John Stanley *Little Lulu #57*
Jim Starlin *Marvel Graphic Novel #1: The Death of Captain Marvel*
Jim Steranko *Incredible Hulk Annual #1, Nick Fury Agent of S.H.I.E.L.D. #4*
Curt Swan *Action Comics #500, Action Comics #583, Adventure Comics #247, Superboy #47, Superman #149, Superman #156, Superman's Girl Friend Lois Lane #19, World's Finest Comics #172*
Arthur Suydam *Marvel Zombies #5*
Romeo Tanghal *Green Lantern (3rd series) #49*
Frank Thorne *Red Sonja #1*
Tim Townsend *New X-Men #114*
Herb Trimpe *Incredible Hulk #181, Incredible Hulk #189*
Uncredited *Classics Illustrated #89, Jeanie #17, Superman #411*
John Verpoorten *Conan the Barbarian #1*
Mike Vosburg *Savage She-Hulk #25*
Ron Wilson *Web of Spider-Man #7*
Barry Windsor-Smith *Conan the Barbarian #1*
Wally Wood *Shock SuspenStories #6, Warfront #37, Weird Science #20*
Bill Wray *Secret Origins #40*
Bernie Wrightson *Swamp Thing #1*
Mike Zeck *Captain America #284*
Dan Zolnerowich *Airboy Comics Vol. 5 #12*

64 *The Greatest Comic Book Covers of All Time*